D0929498

BUNGALOW BASICS
BATHROOMS

By Paul Duchscherer
Photography by Douglas Keister

Pomegranate

SAN FRANCISCO

Published by Pomegranate Communications, Inc.
Box 808022, Petaluma, California 94975
800-227-1428; www.pomegranate.com

Pomegranate Europe Ltd.
Unit 1, Heathcote Business Centre, Hurlbutt Road
Warwick, Warwickshire CV34 6TD, U. K.
44 1926 430111

Library of Congress Cataloging-in-Publication Data
Duchscherer, Paul.
    Bungalow basics. Bathrooms / by Paul Duchscherer ; photography by
Douglas Keister.
        p. cm.
    ISBN 0-7649-2777-9
    1. Bungalows–United States. 2. Bathrooms–United States. 3. Arts and crafts
movement–United States. I. Title: Bathrooms. II. Keister, Douglas. III. Title.

 NA7571.D818 2004
 728'.373–dc22

                                                        2003062205

Pomegranate Catalog No. A702
Designed by Patrice Morris

Printed in Korea

13 12 11 10 09 08 07 06 05 04   10 9 8 7 6 5 4 3 2 1

This book is dedicated to the discovery,
appreciation, and preservation of bungalows,
and especially to all those who
love and care for them.

Acknowledgments

Because of space limitations, we regret that it is not possible to acknowledge each of those individuals and organizations who have helped us with this book. Our heartfelt appreciation is extended especially to all the homeowners who, by graciously sharing their homes with us, have made this book a reality. Special thanks are given also to Sandy Schweitzer, John Freed, and Don Merrill for their tireless support, unflagging encouragement, and invaluable assistance. We salute you!

At the end of the book, we have noted a few of the talented artisans, architects, designers, craftspeople, and manufacturers whose work appears here, but space constraints preclude us from crediting each one. We offer them all our deepest gratitude. Alternatively, our readers may wish to consult the extensive credit listings in our earlier book series, published by Penguin Putnam Inc. (comprising *The Bungalow: America's Arts & Crafts Home, Inside the Bungalow: America's Arts & Crafts Interior,* and *Outside the Bungalow: America's Arts & Crafts Garden*), which make reference to many of the images that are also included in this book.

During the last quarter of the nineteenth century, in response to enlightened national health codes and improved public water and sewer facilities, indoor plumbing gradually became commonplace in most urban American homes. The building industry was quick to incorporate the latest designs of bathroom fixtures and fittings into new housing. Not surprisingly, early-twentieth-century bungalows—considered the most modern homes of the time—had bathrooms that reflected the latest trends and highest standards of efficiency in indoor plumbing.

In a widely applied planning formula, architects and designers gave the bungalow's public areas (living and dining rooms) the lion's share of space, which made it challenging for the tighter utility and private areas to function well. Not as reduced from the more spacious standards of Victorian-era housing as was the kitchen, the bungalow bathroom was generally more than adequate in size (if not downright roomy). Because bungalows typically had only one bathroom—and because families with multiple children constituted a typical bungalow household—the room was subject to nearly constant use. Therefore, its fixtures and finishes had to hold up well to this continuous onslaught, while the room's ongoing cleaning routine had to be as simple as possible.

In general appearance, the earliest twentieth-century bathrooms remained quite similar to the most up-to-date examples of the later nineteenth century. Popularly perceived to be a more "hygienic" color

choice for finishes in service areas, white had dominated most bathroom color schemes before 1900 (Figure 1). It was the standard
color choice for bathroom fixtures, floor and wall tiles, woodwork,
and even wall paint (although some paint schemes incorporated
other pale shades such as cream). This austere sensibility continued
to guide American bathroom design until the 1920s, when more
color started to become fashionable.

Limited by a compact room configuration (and usually a modest
budget), the planning options for locating the bungalow bathroom
were fairly few. One of the most common arrangements placed it and
the two bedrooms off a short hallway, which often was reached
through a door opening to the dining room. In most versions of this
plan, the bathroom was situated between the two bedrooms and
could be entered only from the hall. A second variation allowed for
three doors that opened directly into the bathroom: one from each
bedroom, plus the one connecting to the hall. Another common
arrangement located the bathroom (usually with only one door) at
the far end of a slightly longer hallway. Doors to the bedrooms (and
perhaps another to the kitchen) also opened onto this hall, which
placed the bathroom at the back of the house.

Because of the limited ways that standard-sized plumbing fixtures
could fit into the space, many bungalow bathroom layouts were quite
similar. Bathrooms with access to both the hallway and (at least one of)

the bedrooms tended to be the largest, because they required extra space for the additional door swings (Figure 11). Sometimes a tall, narrow linen closet (or a recessed cabinet), fitted with shelves, also opened into the bathroom (Figure 12). Space permitting, some earlier bungalows incorporated a convenient arrangement called a split bath. The toilet, separate from the tub and sink, was placed in its own private cubicle, with an outside window for light and ventilation. Nicknamed the W.C. (for "water closet"), this narrow compartment was typically located next to the bathroom proper, off the same hall-way. For larger families, this separation allowed for a more efficient use of all the bathroom facilities. Rarely was a bungalow built with two full bathrooms, although a handy extra toilet was sometimes installed in another W.C., usually off the back porch by the kitchen or perhaps in the basement. Today, if a bungalow has two full bath-rooms, one of them was likely a later addition.

Adequate ventilation was a priority, but opportunities for cross-ventilation in bungalow bathrooms were few, as most had only one outside wall. At a minimum, bathrooms contained one or two small, openable windows (Figures 10–13). Some earlier homes boasted a passive ventilation system in the bathroom, which vented warm, moist air through a grille-covered opening in the ceiling into an exhaust pipe through the roof. The metal louvers of the vent could be opened or closed by pulling a hanging chain (Figure 43). Later, built-in electric-powered fans became more widely used (Figures 12, 36). Some larger (and more expensive) bathrooms were heated by a radiator as part of a steam heating system (Figures 31–32) or through a floor vent by a gas furnace (Figure 12), but bathrooms often had no separate heating source at all. Small, built-in gas and electric wall heater units eventually became popular (Figures 19, 28).

Bathroom lighting fixtures came in a fairly limited range of forms and styles. Most early examples were rather plain, utilitarian designs. Larger bathrooms usually had a central ceiling fixture, supplemented by a wall-mounted fixture (or sometimes two) above the sink; in smaller spaces, one or the other of these would suffice. Later bungalow bathrooms, with colorful paint and ceramic tile, were likely to be lit by more stylish fixtures (Figures 21, 24, 27–28).

Plumbing fixtures for most bungalow bathrooms were fairly standard, reflecting what was available on a minimal budget. Most faucets and exposed pipe fittings had a shiny nickel-plated finish, replaced later by chrome plating. Shapely cast-iron pedestal sinks, whose substantial bases shielded unsightly plumbing connections, were a very popular choice (Figures 1, 12, 15, 17–18, 21–26). It was less common (and usually more costly) for earlier sinks to have supporting metal legs (Figures 5, 14). Least expensive—and allowing for unobstructed cleaning underneath—wall-hung cast-iron sinks were also popular and especially useful in bathrooms with restricted space (Figures 11, 13, 20).

A late-Victorian standard, the cast-iron bathtub continued in popularity well into the twentieth century. These freestanding tubs were typically plumbed from the floor and supported on short iron legs with "ball-and-claw" feet, adapted from a late-eighteenth-century carved furniture detail (Figures 4, 7, 13). Extremely affordable because of their mass production over several decades, footed tubs nonetheless presented a challenge when it came time to clean behind and under them. Amateurish attempts to enclose some freestanding tubs (usually with tile-faced wood) in order to circumvent the cleaning issue were mostly unsuccessful. If one could afford it, an early solution to the maintenance problem was a tub with an enclosed base (Figures 1, 8). An attractive variation was the so-called pedestal tub (Figures 15, 17, 43), although most of these were too large for the average bungalow bathroom. As the twentieth century progressed, housewives continued to bemoan the inconvenience of cleaning around footed tubs, and manufacturers eventually responded in the 1920s with less-expensive models that had fully enclosed sides (Figures 18, 20, 22), often designed to be set into corners (Figure 30) or recessed into three-sided alcoves (Figures 23–24, 32). Some enclosed-base tubs had tiling applied directly to their sides (Figures 21, 26).

Innovative freestanding shower units with curtained enclosures were produced in the bungalow's early years, but these were usually too costly, and most couldn't fit into the average bathroom's available space (Figures 5–6). A more common option was a bathtub fitted (or retrofitted) with an overhead shower, shielded by curtains (Figures 8, 13, 43–44). A separate shower stall (in addition to the tub) was a desirable feature, and these became more common from the 1920s onward (Figures 25, 31).

Some early bungalows were equipped with so-called pull-chain toilets, which had wooden seats (usually oak) over porcelain bowls. Mounted high overhead, their wooden water tanks provided a powerful gravity-driven flush (Figure 2). After 1900, toilets that featured a separate but lower water tank, mounted on the wall just above and behind the seat, became a more popular—and quieter—choice; most manufacturers soon adopted their new lower profile (Figures 12, 17). For a time, some of the white porcelain models continued to sport wooden water tanks and seats (Figure 3).

Like the built-ins in the rest of the house, those in the bathroom were probably not custom-built but selected from catalogs and shipped to the site for installation. Nearly every bungalow bathroom had the ubiquitous mirror-faced medicine cabinet over the sink; for good natural light and air, it was often located between a pair of windows (Figures 10–13). If the sink was on an inside wall, the outside wall could be fitted with other cabinetry (Figures 10, 30). Other bathroom built-ins included recessed storage units with various drawers and shelves, and built-in benches with lift-up seats that functioned as laundry hampers (Figure 11). In wide use today, the bathroom vanity (with a sink set into the countertop and an enclosed cabinet underneath) did not become popular until much later (Figures 36, 38).

Compared to that of its living and dining rooms, the budget for finishing the bungalow's secondary spaces was modest. For little cost, enamel paint—typically white or cream—on the bathroom's wood trim could go a long way in unifying its design scheme (Figures 7–9, 14); a slightly contrasting paint color for the walls could enhance the effect (Figures 13, 24). Most bathroom woodwork was painted, although some people did prefer stained finishes. Stenciled borders and throw rugs, also inexpensive, could introduce more color and design elements (Figures 17, 21–22).

The lower and upper wall areas of bathrooms were commonly separated by a wooden molding, which allowed for variations in both the finish material and color of either area (Figure 11). To resist the damaging effects of moisture, the lower portions of bathroom walls generally received a heavy-duty finish, which, at a minimum, meant extra coats of enamel. Another possible treatment for the lower walls, carried over from the Victorian era, was a wainscot made of narrow, interlocking vertical boards (commonly called beadboard or tongue-in-groove paneling), perhaps stained but usually painted (Figure 2). A less costly lower wall treatment simulated the look of ceramic tile by incising the still-wet plaster walls with a grooved pattern (resembling grout lines) prior to painting them. Wallpaper was less typical in bathrooms than elsewhere in the bungalow. So-called sanitary papers, most often in faux tile designs, were widely available; their glossy finish was intended to be varnished after installation, making them an appropriate treatment for the moisture-prone lower walls.

If softwood floors (usually fir) were used in the bathroom, they were often painted with porch-floor enamel to repel water. Higher budgets might allow for a hardwood such as oak or maple (Figure 39). More durable than wood and relatively inexpensive, linoleum flooring could also add color and perhaps a tile-like pattern. Although rare, marble sometimes appeared on the floors and countertops of higher-budget bathrooms (Figures 4–6). Probably the most durable and practical material for bathroom flooring (and certainly one of the most popular) was unglazed white porcelain tile. Its smooth surface was easy to mop, and its grainy finish (and grout lines) made it quite skid-resistant. The most common application of porcelain tile used small (one-inch-wide) hexagonal mosaic tiles to create an overall netlike pattern (Figures 7, 13). Sometimes larger tiles were used, again usually hexagonal (Figures 3, 8). Dark-colored grout worked best with white floor tiles, as it allowed their pattern to stand out and avoided the maintenance pitfalls inherent with discoloration-prone, light-colored grout.

During the bungalow's earlier years, a simple way to add interest to such tiled floors was the addition of a few small accent tiles in a contrasting color (commonly blue or black). Patterned borders, although more costly, could also enliven plain tile floors. Usually composed of one-inch square mosaic tiles, most borders tended to feature simple geometric designs with a minimum of color (Figures 15–16). Generally seen only in more expensive bathrooms of the time, octagonally shaped tiles could be placed in a grid, resulting in a small diagonal square at each intersection—an ideal place for adding an accent color (Figures 1, 4–5). Other mosaic designs incorporated two or more colors of small square or rectangular porcelain tiles into basket weave, herringbone, checkerboard, and other geometric patterns (Figures 18, 26).

Glazed ceramic tile was the most durable and prevalent finish for bathroom walls. Even if the budget was tight, the use of tile on at least the lower wall areas was well worth the added expense. Absolutely essential in shower stalls, it was also highly recommended for walls around tubs fitted with overhead showers. In earlier bathrooms, the most common wall tile was three-by-six-inch white "subway" tile, usually laid in a bricklike "running bond" pattern (Figures 8–9, 12, 15, 19). Some earlier high-budget bathrooms had a decorative border of low-relief tiles running along the top of their subway-tiled wainscots (Figures 1, 4–5). Eventually four-by-four-inch square tiles became the standard for most bathroom walls, which persists today.

By the late 1920s (and continuing long after), the advent of colored porcelain fixtures and a widely expanded range of tile colors and specialty trim pieces gave rise to some of the most dramatic bathrooms ever (Figures 22–23, 26, 29, 30–33). The brighter palette was influenced in part by the Art Deco style, then at the height of its fashion in Europe. Although Art Deco had a far more important influence on America's commercial architecture and on the designs of textiles, furniture, graphics, and mass-produced industrial goods (such as appliances and automobiles), the 1920s and 1930s saw its Jazz Age geometric sensibility show up in many of the shapes and finishes of tiles, lighting, and hardware fittings produced for the residential market (Figures 25, 27–28).

The fact that many bungalow bathrooms have survived with their original fixtures and finishes intact testifies to the quality and durability of the materials used by their builders. Homeowners who are in the process of re-creating an authentic early-twentieth-century bathroom are fortunate to have such models as are featured here. Because others might prefer to create a more contemporary bathroom design for their vintage house, the following pages also include several tasteful remodels to show how others, respecting past traditions and taking new inspiration from them, have succeeded.

❧ 1. Bathroom technology had already made great strides before 1900. This well-equipped bathroom was the result of an 1898 remodel of the Haas-Lilienthal House in San Francisco, a Queen Anne-style Victorian home built in 1886 (now open to the public as a house museum). The finishes and conveniences foreshadow those that would soon become common in more modest early-twentieth-century bathrooms: a pedestal sink, tub (on an enclosed base) with shower, built-in cabinets, and "subway" ceramic wall tile. Except for the accent color, the floor tile treatment in Figure 4 is nearly identical.

❧ 2. *(above, left)* For many years leading up to 1900, so-called pull-chain toilets, with wooden seats and tanks, were a familiar convenience in many American bathrooms. This example, from the 1876 Camron-Stanford House in Oakland, California (open to the public as a house museum), has a porcelain bowl with low-relief ornament, typical of the era. As technology and public taste changed, toilet styles evolved, but wood wainscoting (seen behind) on bathroom walls persisted.

❧ 3. *(above, right)* Original to a 1912 bungalow bathroom, this toilet bears the lower profile and overall form that became increasingly popular after 1900, but it retains the wooden tank and seat of earlier models; however, its push-button flusher was the height of modernity. The wallpaper (a recent addition) adapts a period pattern designed by Dard Hunter for china used at the Roycroft Inn in East Aurora, New York.

4. Footed cast-iron bathtubs were common prior to 1900, and their popularity continued for more than another two decades. The centered plumbing fixtures and squarish shape of this example, from the 1899 Dunsmuir House in Oakland, California (open to the public as a house museum), are typical of a higher-budget bathroom. The room features a marble-slab overflow drain below the tub, a subway-tile wainscot with a low-relief border depicting a shell motif, octagonal white floor tiles with square blue accents, and decorative pinstriping around the tub's sides.

❧ 5. This photograph and the next show shower arrangements in two Dunsmuir House bathrooms, both the result of a remodeling around 1910. This freestanding shower unit has a footed, cast-iron pan and is plumbed with a complex tangle of nickel-plated fittings to mix hot and cold water. A circular ring supports a curtain that surrounds the shower when in use. One of the latest innovations of the time, this model was unaffordable to the average bungalow owner. The marble-topped sink and fancy border on the tiled wainscot also label this bathroom as upscale.

🌀 6. This stall shower is located in another bathroom of Dunsmuir House; it too reflects the most up-to-date (and expensive) plumbing technology then available. In gleaming nickel plate, this "rib-cage" shower was designed to spray its user from the sides as well as from the showerhead above. An early standard feature was a metal-and-glass door (but not an all-marble shower pan, as seen here).

BUNGALOW BASICS

❧ 7. This bathroom in the 1904 house built for C. Hart Merriam (a renowned anthropologist and naturalist) in Marin County, California, retains its original claw-foot tub. The period-inspired sink, tile flooring, and toilet were installed during a recent remodel. A storage compartment is recessed into the board-and-batten paneled walls above the tub. Stepped windows, a result of the roof's slope, allow for better views of the trees from the tub. Light also enters the room from a skylight in a dormer above.

8 & 9. Considered a masterwork of the famous architects Greene and Greene, the 1908 Gamble House in Pasadena, California (open to the public as a house museum), has bathrooms that at first glance appear practical but a bit plain. On closer inspection, their subtly designed woodwork and lighting fixtures reflect the architects' distinctive sensibility. At left, a tub with enclosed sides and a shower (with original nickel-plated plumbing) suggests a higher-budget household, as do the hexagonal floor tiles, which are larger than the most common size. However, the subway wall tiles and sink are fairly standard choices. A detail of a second-floor bathroom (above) shows virtually identical designs for the woodwork (with pegged accents of unpainted oak), medicine cabinet, light fixtures, and tile treatment.

☙ 10. *(above)* This built-in cabinet is an original feature of a 1911 bungalow bathroom whose woodwork was initially painted. Its generous storage includes eight large drawers, four small drawers, two enclosed cupboards (with shelves), and a towering medicine cabinet with a tall mirrored door. Period wall lights (and a pair of windows) illuminate the counter space.

☙ 11. *(right)* Untiled plaster walls in this 1910 bathroom were made considerably more colorful by a recent paint scheme, and the deep green of the wainscot helps unify the space. The door is one of two (at either end) that open directly to bedrooms. All fixtures and features are original; the built-in benches open to reveal laundry hampers.

❧ 12. Original to the 1911 Keyes bungalow in Altadena, California, this extra-roomy bathroom and its sturdy vintage fixtures continue to be practical and efficient today. Familiar amenities include common tile treatments for both floor and walls, a medicine cabinet set between two windows, a built-in linen storage cabinet (far left corner), and a floor heating vent (under chair, lower left). Concealed behind the decorative wood backplate of the ceiling light is a new electric vent.

13. A bathroom in "Mariposa" (formerly the Frost-Tufts House) in Hollywood, California, retains its original 1911 appearance. White fixtures and trim contrast with warm, neutral wall colors. Note the absence of wall tile. The footed tub, wall-hung sink, and small hexagonal floor tiles are all common to the period. Thoughtful extra touches include an adjustable-arm light fixture and a small milk-glass shelf above the sink.

❧ 14. The 1907 Evans House in Marin County, California, was designed by noted local architect Louis C. Mullgardt and remains in the same family who built it. Painted with white enamel, the original board-and-batten paneling of its bathroom sports a fresh look. With original fixtures, the bathroom has a separately compartmented toilet, typical of a "split bath." The sunken bathtub is actually a standard model, recessed into the floor. The so-called sitz bath at right (considered an upgrade at the time) is remembered by the current owner as a good place to bathe children and pets.

15. *(left)* The 1911 Henry Weaver House in Santa Monica, California, is finely detailed throughout. The bathroom is no exception; it manages to be at once simple and elegant. Except for the lighting, all the fixtures, fittings, and finishes are original. The sinuous but substantial pedestal sink pairs nicely with the massive pedestal tub. Most striking is the tiled floor, which features a Greek key motif in its mosaic border.

16. *(right)* This detail shows a floor tile treatment (in a different house) similar to the one in Figure 15. Here the mosaic border is narrower, and it outlines the room's entire perimeter. The pattern is a variation on the Greek key motif, sometimes also called a Greek fret. A scattering of single blue tiles enlivens the overall floor pattern.

◖ 17. From a 1912 catalog published by the Eberson Paint Company, this image was intended to suggest that the utilitarian look of a bathroom could be relieved by paint. Here a cheerful wall color and stenciled border (repeating the colors of the throw rug) offer a pleasing contrast with the white tile and fixtures. While the floor and wall tile treatments, toilet with wall-mounted tank, and pedestal sink reflect an average budget of the period, the leaded-glass window and large pedestal tub are more expensive amenities.

18. The 1923 catalog of the Gordon-Van Tine Company, purveyors of pre-fabricated "kit houses," included this typical model, which listed the following standard features: plumbing fixtures (with nickel-plated fittings); hardware for cabinets, doors, and windows (also nickel-plated); a built-in linen closet; a pair of light fixtures; and wood trim (with enough enamel to give it five coats of paint). Customers had to pay extra for the "minor" fittings–towel bars, cup holder, soap dish, etc.–and the floor and wall tile.

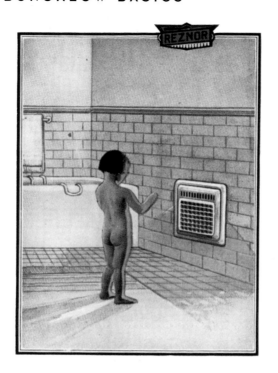

≈ 19. Made graphically clear in this advertising image from the Reznor Manufacturing Company (which appeared in the June 1922 issue of *The Architectural Record*), a gas wall heater could be an effective antidote to a cold bathroom. According to the ad copy, these heaters were made to "harmonize with the finest bathroom fixtures." Electric versions of similarly recessed, small-scale wall heaters were also available.

20. This late-1920s bathroom has a tankless "pressure flush valve" toilet, designed to save water, and a wall-hung sink, favored for tighter spaces–both of which suggest that this view may represent an apartment or hotel setting. The showerless tub's length may define the width of the room. Pattern and color are prominently displayed.

ℭ 21. The wall divisions of this colorful 1920s bathroom appear to be painted, with a wave motif stenciled on top of the wainscot (which seems rather impractical, considering the shower over the tub). The only tile in the entire room is on the sides of the tub. Some tub models were specifically designed to accept tiling on enclosed bases.

🖼 22. A bathroom corner in a 1927 magazine advertisement for Dutch Cleanser features bright white fixtures against a mottled-green glazed tile wainscot. Above it, a stenciled border repeats the firm's logo (a little Dutch girl, who "chases dirt"), which also appears on a bath mat, towel, and (tiny) night-light.

23. *(left)* The tile scheme of this 1920s bathroom is enlivened by a repeating border of water lilies, whose impact is amplified by the adjacent row of plain field tiles in different shades of a similar green. Matching green tiles outline the plain pink fields of the wainscot and diagonally set floor tiles. The steel sash window is original.

24. *(above)* A 1927 magazine advertisement for plumbing fixtures shows a bathtub with an enclosed base, set into a three-sided alcove. Although the choice of white for both tile and fixtures was still prevalent (and least expensive) at this date, the image attests to the increasing emphasis on color in bathrooms.

€ 25. *(left)* This bathroom was installed around 1930 between two attic-level bedrooms of a bungalow that was built about a decade earlier. The shiny black tile walls and geometric accents give it a snazzy Art Deco flair. The black presents a dramatic contrast to the pale "Nile green" fixtures and various accent tiles, some of which have a metallic gold glaze. A built-in shower stall (at right) takes the place of a bathtub.

€ 26. *(above)* By the late 1920s, the use of color, pattern, and lots of tile was to be expected in a tile manufacturer's advertisement. Although the fixtures remain white, this bathroom makes a bolder tile statement than it would have earlier in the same decade. Rose walls above the tile and a deep plum rug with a border introduce more color.

27 & 28. A recent, hand-painted Art Deco-style mural of a surreal underwater world is this 1925 bathroom's most striking feature. Crisply outlined in white, the shell-pink tile wainscot provides a tailored contrast. Tiny pink porcelain mosaic tiles, also with a white border, cover the floor. A vintage freestanding circular aquarium looks very much at home. Under the leaded art-glass window is a white wall heater. A double border of white tile frames the medicine cabinet, whose mirror (in the photograph above) reflects the mural's metallic silver paint and the higher tiling around the tub area. Period Art Deco lighting blends utility with Jazz Age style.

❧ 29. *(left)* In an outlandishly colorful bathroom from the late 1920s, orchid-colored wall tiles are framed by a deep shade of jade green in the trim that surrounds the door and defines the upper walls. A tile border with stylized designs combines two shades of the same green with mauve accents. Such vivid schemes were then perceived as the height of fashion.

❧ 30. *(right)* The softened edges of the coved ceiling echo those of the comfortably rounded, original cast-iron tub fitted in the corner of a 1925 bathroom. While the pedestal sink is a replacement, the original medicine cabinet and built-in dressing table on the window wall survive. Outlined with a black border (barely distinguishable from the deep shades of blue), the floor tiles are set in a lively geometric pattern. The blue-green field tiles of the wainscot, also bordered in black, inject a brighter shot of color.

❦ 31 & 32. These two similarly configured bathrooms are original to the same house, a 1927 Spanish Colonial Revival. Built for Walter P. Temple, "La Casa Nueva" is now open to the public as part of the Workman and Temple Family Homestead Museum, in City of Industry, California. Despite identical plumbing fixtures and heater grilles, their varying tile and color schemes make each room quite distinct. In Figure 32 (above), the floor and wall tiles are corresponding shades of green, making the space feel larger. Unlike the regular grid pattern of the floor, the wainscot's field comprises two tile sizes, placed to align with the grout lines of the unusual tile border design. The cutaway detail of the border, with curving swags connecting stylized floral forms, helps soften the room's hard edges. The tile color and arrangement in Figure 31 (left) are more typical and more akin to the house's style. Terra-cotta floor tile, bordered in black, helps anchor the brighter orange of the wainscot. On a more delicate scale, the accent border's lively pattern introduces additional color.

33. The result of a 1930s remodel, the bathroom plumbing fixtures in a 1914 bungalow are the same shade of green seen in Figure 25. Sometimes called Nile green, or *eau de Nil* (water of the Nile), this color became popular after the 1922 discovery of King Tutankhamen's tomb, which influenced the Art Deco style. Darker and lighter shades of a similar green were selected for the new tile scheme; the wainscot has a thin low-relief accent border. To set off the fixtures, the floor tile is mostly white.

❧ 34 & 35. *(overleaf)* Two bathrooms on different floors of a Portland, Oregon, bungalow were remodeled to reflect more of an Arts and Crafts aesthetic. The "Honeysuckle" wallpaper, designed in 1883 by May Morris (daughter of England's great William Morris), dominates the first-floor (guest) bathroom. Below its period-style medicine cabinet and lighting, a tile backsplash lends a vintage look to a modern sink. The flooring and base trim are made of natural slate. A new low wall helps conceal the toilet. In the upstairs (family) bathroom, walls painted sage green are a soothing foil for the white woodwork, fixtures, and new built-in cabinets. The linoleum floor and decorative tile backsplash above the sink (similar to the one in the downstairs bathroom) are also new additions.

❧ 36. *(right)* The remodel of a circa-1900 house gave the opportunity for this interpretation of a period-style bathroom, a creative assemblage of old and new. "Recycled" vintage elements include the sink and rose marble surround, faucets, leaded art-glass panels, and cast-iron heating grilles (used to cover the ceiling light and fan). The tile wainscot in the tub alcove is made with pieces of matte-glazed floor tile, which was specially cut and installed to mimic the adjacent wood wainscoting.

❧ 37. Opening onto a small, private, covered deck with views into towering evergreens, this bathroom was part of a recent addition to a picturesque 1910 log house near Seattle. To be closer to nature, a freestanding tub has been positioned under a window, framed by tall cascades of draperies. A reconditioned classic, the tub is outfitted with ball-and-claw feet, period-style hardware, and exposed plumbing connections. Slate flooring is a practical choice, in keeping with the home's rustic feeling.

⌒ 38 (& detail). Pictured in Figures 38 and 39 are bathrooms in a bungalow that recently underwent extensive renovations. This photograph and detail image show what was created within the space of the original bathroom. Now used as the guest bath, the room features extensive quartersawn oak cabinetry, handmade copper hardware, a marble countertop, and fine period lighting. Seen in the mirror, an open shower door reveals a hand-painted tile mural, which covers the shower's entire back wall.

⬤ 39 (& detail). In the same remodeled bungalow, this view (from the master bedroom) looks through the new dressing room into the master bathroom; both areas were the result of a creative reassignment of existing bedroom space. With vintage lighting, the dressing room has a built-in vanity and mirror, opposite a closet. Quartersawn oak was used for the cabinetry and hardwood flooring, which is inlaid with strips of walnut to form a popular period design. An enormous footed tub beckons in the bathroom beyond. The room is lit by a Tiffany art-glass globe, which inspired the colors and geometric patterns of the tile.

40. This second-floor bathroom was remodeled to allow a claw-foot tub to be placed within a light-filled bay window, surrounded by greenery. The period-style built-in cabinet was designed to resemble a piece of freestanding furniture. A new tile wainscot adds a subdued color statement and helps anchor the sloped ceiling.

41. Published in a bungalow plan book in the 1910s, this illustration has several features in common with the next example (shown in Figures 42–43), most notably the decorative painting concept for a bathroom frieze. The toilet and tiled wainscot treatment are nearly identical with those in the Lanterman House bathroom, but a more typical bathtub and wall-hung sink appear here. Considered especially suitable for a bathroom, the aquatic theme of the frieze uses foreground sprays of bamboo to divide alternating scenes of animated swans and tranquil water lilies.

🌿 42 & 43. Before and after views of a bathroom in the 1915 Lanterman House in La Cañada-Flintridge, California (open to the public as a house museum), show the transformation made by cleaning and restoration of the original hand-painted frieze above the tile wainscot. A watery landscape is suggested by the motif of irises, which sprout in clumps at strategic points around the room. Other higher-budget items are the pedestal tub with original shower fittings (including a circular curtain rod), fluted white pedestal sink, and louvered ventilation shaft (operated by a pull-chain above the toilet). More "textbook" examples of period design include the hexagonal floor tiles and three-by-six-inch wall tiles.

✿ 44 & 45. Before and after views of a bathroom in a 1914 bungalow illustrate the restoration of original design elements that had been lost to a previous remodel. As shown in the earlier photograph (above), only one of two small double-hung windows that had once flanked the medicine cabinet remained; the other window had been covered over to allow for plumbing of a shower and tiling of the walls over the tub. Most traces of the original floor and wall tile, lighting, and plumbing fixtures had also vanished. Bulky cabinetry (not original) crowded the space. The later view (right) shows that the owner has restored not only the missing window but also period-style lighting, hexagonal porcelain floor tile, and a glazed subway-tile wainscot. A new pedestal sink has been installed, along with a vintage footed tub fitted with a shower and a curtain rod secured to the ceiling. An unusual shade of lavender on the wood trim (to match the vintage hooked rug) and dark navy blue paint on the sides and feet of the tub add color to the mostly white room.

BUNGALOW BACKGROUND

America's most popular house of the early twentieth century, the bungalow, is making a big comeback as our newest "historic" house. Surviving bungalows are now considered treasures by historic preservationists, while homeowners rediscover the bungalow's appeal as a modest, practical home with a convenient floor plan. This book highlights an important aspect of bungalow interiors.

Webster's New Collegiate Dictionary describes a bungalow as "a dwelling of a type first developed in India, usually one story, with low sweeping lines and a wide verandah." The word *bungalow* derives from the Hindi *bangala,* both an old Hindu kingdom in the Bengal region of India and a rural Bengali hut with a high thatched-roof overhang creating a covered porch (or verandah) around the perimeter to provide shade from the scorching sun. The height and steep pitch of the roof encouraged the hottest air to rise and escape, while cooler air flowed in at ground level (especially after sundown). The British colonists adapted the design in their own dwellings, and their success spread the concept from India to elsewhere in the British Empire, especially Southeast Asia, Africa, New Zealand, and Australia. By the late eighteenth century, the name *bangala* had been anglicized to *bungalow.*

This name first appeared in print in the United States in 1880.

Used in an architectural journal, it described a single-story, shingled Cape Cod summerhouse ringed by covered porches. By the 1900s, *bungalow* had become part of our popular vocabulary, at first associated with vacation homes, both seaside and mountain. The bungalow's informality, a refreshing contrast to stuffy Victorian houses, helped fuel its popularity as a year-round home. It had its greatest fame as a modest middle-class house from 1900 to 1930.

Widely promoted, the bungalow was touted for its modernity, practicality, affordability, convenience, and often-artistic design. Expanding industry and a favorable economy across the country created an urgent need for new, affordable, middle-class housing, which the bungalow was just in time to meet.

In America, a bungalow implied a basic plan, rather than a specific style, of modest house. Typically, it consisted of 1,200 to 1,500 square feet, with living room, dining room, kitchen, two bedrooms, and bathroom all on one level. Some bungalows had roomy attic quarters, but most attics were bare or intended to be developed as the family's needs grew. A bungalow set in a garden fulfilled many Americans' dream of a home of their own.

Widely publicized California bungalows in the early 1900s spawned frenzied construction in booming urban areas across the country. In design, most bungalows built prior to World War I adopted the so-called Craftsman style, sometimes combined with influences from the Orient, the Swiss chalet, or the Prairie style. After the war, public taste shifted toward historic housing styles, and bungalows adapted Colonial Revival, English cottage, Tudor, Mission, and Spanish Colonial Revival features.

Today Craftsman is the style most associated with bungalows. Characterized inside and out by use of simple horizontal lines, Craftsman style relies on the artistry of exposed wood joinery (often visible on front porch detailing). Natural or rustic materials (wood siding, shingles, stone, and clinker brick) are favored. Interiors may be enriched with beamed ceilings, high wainscot paneling, art glass, and hammered copper or metalwork lighting accents.

The word *Craftsman* was coined by prominent furniture manufacturer and tastemaker Gustav Stickley, who used it to label his line of sturdy, slat-backed furniture (also widely known as Mission style), which was influenced by the English Arts and Crafts movement. That movement developed in the mid-nineteenth century as a reaction against the Industrial Revolution. Early leaders such as John Ruskin and William Morris turned to the medieval past for inspiration as they sought to preserve craft skills disappearing in the wake of factory mechanization.

In both the decorative arts (furniture, wallpaper, textiles, glass, metalwork, and ceramics) and architecture, the Arts and Crafts movement advocated use of the finest natural materials to make practical and beautiful designs, executed with skillful handcraftsmanship. One goal was to improve the poor-quality, mass-produced home furnishings available to the rising middle class. Morris and a group of like-minded friends founded a business to produce well-designed, handcrafted goods for domestic interiors. Although the company aspired to make its goods affordable to all, it faced the inevitable conflict between quality and cost. However, its Arts and Crafts example inspired many others in England (and eventually in America) to relearn treasured old craft traditions and continue them for posterity.

As it grew, the movement also became involved in politics, pressing for social reforms. Factory workers trapped in dull, repetitive jobs (with little hope for anything better) were among their chief concerns; they saw the workers' fate as a waste of human potential and talent.

The idealistic and visionary English movement's artistic goals of design reform were more successful than its forays into social reform. Perhaps its greatest success, in both England and the United States, was in giving the public a renewed sense of the value of quality materials, fine craftsmanship, and good design in times of rapid world change.

The Arts and Crafts movement had multiple influences on the American bungalow. The movement arrived here from England in the early 1900s, just as the bungalow was becoming popular. Among its most successful promoters was Elbert Hubbard, founder of the Roycroft Community, a group of artisans producing handmade books and decorative arts inspired by Morris. Hubbard also published two periodicals and sold goods by mail order.

Gustav Stickley was another American inspired by England's important reform movement and soon was expressing this inspiration in the sometimes austere but well-made designs of his Craftsman style. Becoming an influential promoter of the bungalow as an ideal "Craftsman home," he marketed furniture, lighting, metalwork, and textiles styled appropriately for it. His magazine, *The Craftsman,* was a popular vehicle for his ideas and products, and he sold plans for the Craftsman houses he published in his magazine. The wide popularity of his Craftsman style spread the aesthetic sensibilities of the Arts and Crafts movement into countless American middle-class households, making it a growing influence on architecture and decorative arts here. (England in the early twentieth century remarkably had no middle-class housing form comparable to the American bungalow, but Australia has bungalows of that period, inspired by ours, rather than any from Britain.)

Other manufacturers eventually contributed to Stickley's downfall by blatantly copying his ideas and products and eroding his market share. Once Stickley's exclusive brand name, the word *Craftsman* was assimilated into general use and became public property after his bankruptcy in 1916.

Americans choosing the Craftsman style for their homes, interiors, and furnishings rarely were committed to the artistic and philosophical reforms of the Arts and Crafts movement; most were simply following a vogue. Prospective homeowners (and real estate developers) usually selected their bungalow designs from inexpensive sets of plans marketed in catalogs called plan books; few used an architect's services. Some people even bought prefabricated "ready-cut" or "kit" houses. First sold in 1909 by Sears, Roebuck and Company, prefabricated houses soon were widely copied. In the heat of bungalow mania, Sears and others offered tempting incentives to prospective bungalow buyers, such as bonus financing for their lots. For a time, it was said that if you had a job, you could afford a bungalow. But when jobs were in short supply as the Great Depression hit, many defaulted on their little dream homes, leaving their creditors stung.

The depression ended the heyday of the bungalow, but its practical innovations reappeared in later houses, then more likely to be called cottages. The post-World War II ranch house could be considered the legacy of the bungalow. Only recently has a rising demand for lower-cost houses triggered a reevaluation of vintage bungalow stock as viable housing. In response to public demand, the home planning and construction industries have reprised some of the obvious charms of the bungalow in new homes. A real boon for homeowners seeking to restore or renovate a vintage bungalow (or perhaps build a new one) is today's flourishing Arts and Crafts revival, fueled by the demand for a wide array of newly crafted home furnishings that reflect the traditions and spirit of the Arts and Crafts movement. ℭ

CREDITS

Figure 3: Wallpaper from Roycroft Shops, Inc. **Figure 7:** Sink and toilet from Sunrise Salvage; light from Omega Salvage. **Figure 10:** Restoration contractor: Elder Vides. **Figure 13:** Restoration architect: Martin Eli Weil. **Figure 33:** Tile by Pratt and Larson; lighting by Rejuvenation Lamp and Fixture Company. **Figures 34–35:** Wallpaper by Arthur Sanderson and Sons; tile and slate by Pratt and Larson; lighting by Rejuvenation Lamp and Fixture Company. **Figure 36:** Interior design and wall sconces by John Zanakis, House of Orange; design consultant and finish carpentry: Timothy Hansen; wainscot tile by Heath Ceramics; grilles for ceiling fan and light by Reggio Register. **Figure 37:** Renovation architect: Robert I. Hoshide, Hoshide Williams; project architect: Grace Schlitt. **Figures 38–39:** General contractor: Marshall White Construction; cabinetry by Mike Marnell; hardware by Buffalo Studios; period lighting from Mike Collier; tile mural painted by Brenda Rose; floor and wall field tile by Architerra Northwest Tile; tile borders by Dale Marsh, Tile Artisans. **Figure 40:** Interior design by Valerie Olsen. **Figure 43:** Restoration consultant: John Benriter; wall painting restoration by Pinson and Ware, Landmark Painted Design and Restoration. **Figure 45:** General contractor: Dean Poppe; tub from Omega Salvage; lighting by Rejuvenation Lamp and Fixture Company.

ARCHIVAL IMAGES

Figure 17: Courtesy the collection of Dianne Ayres and Timothy Hansen, Arts & Crafts Period Textiles. **Figures 19–22, 24, 26:** From the collection of Paul Duchscherer. **Figures 18, 41:** Courtesy of Dover Publications, Inc.